GOOD FINISH *to* BAD START

SAM O. ADEWUNMI

Opportunities are missed because we look at the enormity of our challenges ... page 84

I pray that this book will positively impact your life. Thank you for attending the book launch and God bless.

Sam O. Adewunmi

www.pastorsam.tv

COVENANT PUBLISHING

Good Finish to Bad Start
Sam Adewunmi

Unless otherwise stated, all scripture quotations are taken from the Holy Bible, New King James Version (NKJV). Other versions cited are NIV, KJV, GNB, God's Word and NLT.

ISBN 978-1-907734-44-1
First Edition
First Printing January 2013

Covenant Publishing
samadewunmi@btinternet.com

Covenant Publishing is part of New Covenant Church
Charity Registered in England & Wales number 1004343
Registered Address: 506-510 Old Kent Road. LONDON SE1 5BA

Cover Design by Covenant Publishing Team
Sam Adewunmi's photo by David Adetoye
Published by Covenant Publishing
Printed in the United Kingdom

ENDORSEMENTS

Good Finish to Bad Start sounds to me like 'there is hope for you.' And that is the message in this book, that whatever wrong turns you may have taken in life until now, you can turn things around. Not only does this book offer hope, it gives you a plan for executing your turn-around experience.

Pastor Sam is a sound teacher. Good Finish to Bad Start is written in an easy-to-understand style, so I encourage you to develop and write down your action steps as you read along.

Great! We're ready to go. Don't drop this book without deciding that you will give life your very best shot. That is a good place to start. Happy reading!

Sam Adeyemi

Pastor, Author & Host 'Success Power International'

With white hot passion, no nonsense directness, unequivocal frankness and absolute clarity, Pastor Sam delivers sound, sensible, pragmatic and down to earth life truths that are difficult to ignore in Good Finish to Bad Start. He uses thought provoking and hard to forget anecdotes to drive his point home; and he makes biblical truths accessible to everyday living.

This book is many resources rolled into one. It is a time management manual, a financial empowerment handbook, a personal motivational bible, a life coaching workbook and a Spirit-led living guidebook all at the same time. Whatever your story, no matter how poorly you started out in life; Pastor Sam flat out tells you that you have no excuse for finishing poorly.

Dr Tayo Adeyemi

Senior Pastor, New Wine Church UK

God does not make failures, so everyone is born with the potential to succeed and end well in life. He does not also require of people what they are incapable of, so he equips us to succeed. Part of the equipping is the people he has placed in our lives to nurture, nourish and build us up in various ways. Having worked closely with Reverend Sam Adewunmi for many years, I am convinced he is one of those assigned to build up people to succeed in life.

Whatever stage you are at the moment in your journey in life, this book will help you along in the process of finishing well.

Femi Omisade

National Overseer, New Covenant Church UK

I have been inspired reading the book Good Finish To Bad Start. Now I have a scriptural backing for what

I've always believed that christian young men should marry in their mid twenties and seize life early.

Citing biblical, classical and contemporary sources, Pastor Sam engages readers in a captivating message of hope. In a light to read, but dense on wisdom and insight approach, he woos you to finish with a bang, whether you started from a bad, better or the best background. I highly recommend to you a book which I believe to be highly inspirational, without reservation.

Dr T. Ayodele Ajayi

General Adult Psychiatrist;

Member of the Royal College of Psychiatrists;

Author 'Footprints of Giants'

Reading the book, 'Good Finish to Bad Start,' was a delight to my soul. It is filled with nuggets of wisdom that is bound not only to inspire and inform you but also to propel you to become the best you can be in life. No matter how bad your beginning was, you can still rewrite your history. I not only celebrate my brother, Pastor Sam, but I encourage everyone both leaders and the led to read this book

Wale Babatunde

Senior Minister, World Harvest Christian Centre (UK)

One of the things I have come to realise about life is that, this is the real thing; there is no practice session before joining the big game. This is it. This is the big game. In many cases, people realise they are in the big game far too late. They squander opportunities, misuse their time, squander money, destroy relationships and suffer the determined consequences of leading such a reckless life. This is why we need some help to learn how to redeem time, plan ahead, be focussed, work diligently and have a burning trust in God - all of which are offerings from this book. Sam Adewunmi's critical analysis, down to earth examples and on-the-ball analogies makes this book a life changing, yet entertaining read.

The author's impassioned plea, encouragement, cajoling and soft nudging to see people and their lives transformed is evident as you read the book. What better describes his heart than the title of the book itself – 'Good Finish To Bad Start'. In other words, though you may start badly, you can still have a good finish. Go on and finish good.

Gbenga Badejo

Principal Partner Park Royal &

Lagos Finishing School (UK & Nigeria)

Pastor Sam in this book has really painted, in a well written form, what everyone has been trying to say for a long time. It is not about opportunity, it is about having an eye for it, the ability to identify it, run with it and obtain, retain and maintain it. This book will be beneficial to everyone wanting to map out their steps towards a successful future.

Tayo Arowojolu

Pastor & Author 'Make That Move Right Now'

A compelling read which helps the reader develop tomorrows realities today. No matter what stage of life you are, this book will inspire and enable you to realise that your today and tomorrow can be much better than your past.

It is a much held belief that life opportunities once lost can never be actualised again. Good Finish to Bad Start enables one to realise that opportunities will always avail themselves to a person throughout ones lifetime, irrespective of past failures.

This book goes a step further by enabling the reader to identify general opportunities and pitfalls of life.

The author is studious in encouraging readers to plan and strategise the present and future time. For some chances will be as a result of written down ideas and projections.

Tayo Yemi

Pastor, New Covenant Church Barcelona (Spain)

This book by Pastor Sam is a multi-channel cutting edge tool for anyone that desires to become a high flyer in life. The author has released many solutions to most of the everyday-desire and need of everyday-man. It answers most of the questions that place a limitation in people's life, ranging from spiritual, financial, and social. Reading, I noticed that from beginning to the end the book is loaded with secrets of life that can increase the value of anyone that takes time to read and study through. The book will help you learn how to go through the process of your life's purpose to fulfil your dreams.

I am also grateful to God for the author's skilful approach in writing in such a way that reaches everybody at any level of life. Wherever you are in your walk with the Lord, in your financial and business life, ministry or whatever vocation you find yourself, the Golding pages of this book has something positive to offer to you. If you want to take your life's assignment to another level, I guarantee that reading this book will unlock the secrets of the 'next-level' blessings upon your life. You will receive divine energy for unlimited blessings.

All you need in life to be fulfilled is the wisdom of how to move forward from any situations of limitation to the realm of success. GOOD FINISH to BAD START– That is what this book is also about. You will discover how to move from zero to hero, how to move from nobody to somebody, and how to walk into your destiny without any limitations. Applying the simple practical keys in this book will help you maximize the time you have here on earth.

I heartily recommend this book to anybody that desires to have a balance in their life's assignment to bring the fulfilment that comes from our Father of mercy and grace.

Dr James O Nanjo, Pastor

Author & Pastor Restoration Chapel International (UK)

Good Finish To Bad Start reveals an in-depth expression of God's heart for our generation. Pastor Sam unravels the deficient and asthenic mindset of thinking and reasoning which stops us human from taking charge of our own lives but would rather put the blame on other things such as our genetics, relationships and experiences in life.

I was more than excited when in the third chapter "The Morning of Life" he uprooted the fundamental issue that plagues our society including the church today about the lack of investment into the lives of our children and youth at the most productive time of their lives when we are able to impact their beliefs and understanding. I am aware that only a meagre percentage of the church resources are invested into the lives of our children, so a quick reminder that our ministry starts from our home and not the church or mission field is a point worth thinking about.

Reverend Adewunmi in this book was able to highlight the need for parents to invest not just money but time and emotions into the lives of their children. I also got an understanding that parents need to consider raising their children as both a privilege and a responsibility that has divine backing, and as such need to take such roles seriously so as not to miss the crucial period of valuable impaction.

The book has addressed very key issues about raising our children properly and balancing this with scriptural guidance while not breaking the law of the land in regards to safe guarding issues which I consider wide societal problem.

I recommend this book to every person, young or old who is ready to confront their inadequacies and begin to reposition themselves to face the truth of life and relocate themselves to where God has scripted them to be in life by making use of opportunities around them and using their time wisely.

Dr Olaniyi Ajayi MBChB, MSc

Senior Specialist medical practitioner in

Addiction Psychiatry (UK)

TABLE OF CONTENTS

Dedication

To God and all who understands
what it means to fall

Foreword

Some ministers write books because they feel it's their ministry. Others write because they want to be able to say they have written books, just like their peers. I feel this book, however, is written because the author has a vast knowledge of his subject. More importantly he feels a sense of compulsion to share his experiences and observation.

I would encourage you to read the book. For I have read the author, the man himself, over a period of 20 years as a member of our church and now member of its leadership. What he says is little compared to what he has seen. And he has seen a lot.

Paul Jinadu
General Overseer
New Covenant Church

INTRODUCTION

Don't Sell Out

INTRODUCTION

Don't Sell Out

I want to tell you the story of the prodigal son. The story can be found in the Gospel according to Luke, chapter fifteen, and verses eleven through to thirtytwo.

There was a wealthy man who had two sons. The younger demanded to have his inheritance while his father was still alive.

> *"In this case of a will it is necessary to prove that the person who made it has died, for a will means nothing while the person who made it is alive; it goes into effect only after his death"* (Hebrews 9:16-17, GNB).

Against his wish and the customs of the elders, the father gave unto him a portion of the inheritance.

The young man packed his bags and travelled to the ends of the earth and squandered his future. At his destination, the economy became depressed and the standard of living went up. Things became unaffordable so he started living rough. After a long time of suffering alone, he decided to hook up with a citizen so they could share the mounting burden together. Things grew even worse and he began to feed on pod meant for swine on the field where he got a part time job. When he could no longer bear the pain of the hard life, he came back to his senses and decided to swallow his pride and return home as a servant.

He returned home hoping to work and be paid just like any servant in the house but ran into the embrace of his waiting father who with good grace offered him pardon.

The lives of many people today resemble that of

this prodigal. When they should be pursuing worthwhile projects, they run after immediate and temporary gratification.

The devil still uses the same strategies today. He has not changed. He often convinces people it's not necessary to be serious about the things of God. He lulls people into a fake sense of security and makes believing God look stupid.

He is in the business of stopping people making their destiny. He will use money, sex, fame, pride, laziness, illness, and whatever else is available at his disposal to make sure people do not fulfill their destiny.

He will try to convince people that using drugs, taking alcohol or smoking is okay. He will tell people it is okay to have sex before marriage or be unfaithful to their spouse saying something like this: "after all God is merciful and compassionate, He sure will forgive if you repent". From taking such risks, many people have met with their end without repenting.

He finally targets the heart or soul. He makes people fear the future. He uses worldly pleasure and hopes of wealth to enslave people. Today, many people's god is money and their church is work. But God says,

> *"No servant can be the slave of two masters; such a slave will hate one and love the other or will be loyal to one and despise the other. You cannot serve both God and money"* (Luke 16:13, GNB).

Over the past eighteen years, I have seen a number of my Christian friends drop out of the race. They got trapped in the futile pursuit of worldly pleasures. Many started Christian fellowships, others pioneered churches, while others joined existing vibrant congregations. There was fire burning in their bones. They required no convincing to do any assignment. They were unstoppable. We organised outreaches together, played in the Christian Football League and won three successive victory trophies. We joined together in organising our weddings and receptions. We were going to take the city for Jesus.

Unfortunately, one by one they dropped off, their flames extinguished. I have watched how out of frustration, loss of focus and the devil's distractions, many of my friends have abandoned the passion and commitment they used to have. They lived like they had eternity to enjoy and would never grow old or weary.

But I have good news for you. This book is written to encourage those who have given up hope concerning their future not to give up. You may have had a poor start but you can still have a good finish. You can still rise up, better your life, and help the generation coming behind.

This is not a book for the fainthearted or those who just want to pass through life as a statistic. It is a book for the brave, bold, courageous and spirited; those who want to live life knowing time is redeemable but life is irreplaceable; those who are not waiting for life to happen to them but are ready to take it by the horns and ride on the platform of living than just existing. Though life deals them a great blow, they muster their energy to get back up and face life again.

I encourage you to carry on reading if you are ready to take charge of life by the help of God. Adam failed to take charge of life and he lost dominion in the Garden of Eden. Cain did not take charge of his life; he became a murderer and a wanderer. Noah and Abraham took charge and they impacted their world. If you must finish well, you need to take charge of the rest of your life. Have a good read.

CHAPTER 1

Maximise the Moment

CHAPTER 1

Maximise the Moment

Friends of George Burns have always kidded him about his singing. Burns, a master of self-deprecating humour, decided to take advantage of this and insure his voice for a million dollars. He thought it would be a wonderful publicity stunt. "I was so excited," said Burns, "I couldn't wait to rush down to the insurance company. I took a cassette and a tape recorder with me so the insurance man could hear my voice. It was one of my best numbers - a syncopated version of Yankee Doodle Blues with a yodelling finish. The insurance man listened patiently to the whole thing, and then he just looked at me and said, 'Mr. Burns, you should have come to us before you had the accident.'"[i]

George Burns was too late.

Who you are today could be a result of what happened to you yesterday. What you will become tomorrow could be determined by the choices you make today. What happened yesterday may not be your fault but what you become tomorrow is your responsibility. You can blame somebody for pushing you down but you can only blame yourself for staying down. Whatever you sow, you will reap. So, what you do today will affect your tomorrow.

You can blame somebody for pushing you down but you can only blame yourself for staying down.

A farm boy accidentally overturned his wagonload of corn in the road. The farmer who lived nearby came to investigate. "Hey, Willis," he called out. "That's mighty nice of you," Willis answered, "But I don't think Pa would like me to."

"Aw, come on, son!" the farmer insisted.

"Well, okay," the boy finally agreed, "but Pa won't like it."

After a hearty dinner, Willis thanked his host. "I feel a lot better now, but I just know Pa is going to be real upset."

"Don't be foolish!" exclaimed the neighbour. "By the way, where is he?"

"Under the wagon."

Many people leave their problems under the wagon and pursue after temporary pleasures. They miss their opportunity.

BORN WITH A SILVER SPOON

I looked at the top 10 richest men in the world in October 2012, and like many years before, only 2 of them made their wealth from inheritance. Four-fifths were self-made. It's true to say that no one is born rich.[ii]

"After all, we didn't bring any money with us when we came into this world, and we can't carry away a single penny when we die" (I Timothy 6:7, TLB).

Job said,

"I was born with nothing, and I will die with nothing" (Job 1:21, GNB).

Whether you were born in a royal or general hospital, naturally or with help of surgery, in a developing or developed nation, all of us were born naked and empty. We all brought nothing into this world; all of us in a sense are equal. So we can say God is good and very impartial.

No one is born with a silver spoon in their mouth. Those who inherited wealth were given silver spoons after they are born into families of people who laboured ahead of them to acquire the spoon and accumulate the wealth.

Millions of people live in and by the legacy of their parents' fortunes. But there's nothing like becoming a self-made man. Very few people read books written by people who inherited their wealth but books written by self-made millionaires are instant best sellers.

ALL ARE EQUAL

"[10]Whatever you do, do well. For when you go to the grave, there will be no work or planning or knowledge or wisdom. [11]I have observed something else in this world of ours. The fastest runner doesn't always win the race, and the strongest warrior doesn't always win the battle. The wise are often poor, and the skillful are not necessarily wealthy. And those who are educated don't always lead successful lives. [12]It is all decided by chance, by being at the right place at the right time. People can never predict when hard times might come. Like fish in a net or birds in a snare, people are often caught by sudden tragedy" (Ecclesiastes 9:10-12, NLT).

Work now because when you die, you cannot work anymore. That's the message in the passage and the summary of the tenth verse. Coming to verse eleven, we can say; making it in life has little to do with our swiftness, strength, intelligence, wit, or how good we are. The fastest runner doesn't always win the race, and the strongest warrior doesn't always win the battle. The wise are often poor, and the skillful are not necessarily wealthy. And those who are educated don't always lead successful lives. Doesn't that sound familiar? Let me remind you what it concludes:

Making it in life has little to do with our swiftness, strength, intelligence, wit, or how good we are.

> *"... It is all decided by chance, by being at the right place at the right time"* (Ecclesiastes 9:11, NLT).

That sounded like a contradiction. If making it in life is a result of right positioning and right timing, it suffices to say that it cannot be left to chance. So for the rest of this section, we will try to understand this statement and see how it applies to our lives.

The word 'chance' used in this passage may be a little confusing. I say this because it will suggest uncertainty. It may also suggest coincidence. This is not what it means. God is not a God of chance or of coincidences. Everything He does is preordained and planned. The statement 'by being at the right place' means things do not happen accidentally or randomly. If you are not at the right place at the right time, you might miss your chance.

The Hebrew word translated 'chance' is the word 'pega' which means occurrence or happening. It speaks of an incident or event rather than an accident. It is from the root word 'paga' which means; to encounter, meet, reach, entreat, or make intercession.

An alternate word would be 'opportunity.' So from now on I will be using the word 'opportunity.' Let's now replace the word 'chance' with the word 'opportunity' in the NKJV and see how it reads:

> *"I returned and saw under the sun that - the race is not to the swift, nor the battle to the strong, nor bread to the wise, nor riches to men of understanding, nor favour to men of skill; BUT TIME AND OPPORTUNITY HAPPEN TO THEM ALL. For man also does not know his time: like fish taken in a cruel net, like birds caught in a snare, so the sons of men are snared in an evil time, when it falls suddenly upon them"* (Ecclesiastes 9:11-12, Emphasis mine).

If agility, strength, wisdom, education or ability does not make a person, what will? My answer is simple; TIME and OPPORTUNITIES. What makes the difference between your making it in life or otherwise is how you spend your time and take advantage of the opportunities that come your way. This is why I said earlier on that God is fair. He is good and impartial. No one will stand before Him in judgement to say he didn't make it because he was not born into a rich family or nation. The worlds 10 richest billionaires used their time and opportunities wisely to create or increase their wealth. Most are from poor families and nations and represent all age groups. Some did not have a good start, but they changed their fortunes by seizing the moment. They were not going to settle for a bad start and a bad finish.

Since we came to this world with nothing, God gave us time and opportunities fairly. If you pay close attention to how you spend your time and grab the opportunities that God brings your way, you will be fulfilled and make it in life.

WHAT AN OPPORTUNITY!

God gives to everyone a measure of time and plenty of opportunities. Within your time frame, there are ample windows of opportunities. We don't create opportunities for ourselves; God does, using other people. You can desire it but you cannot create it. After you desire it, you wait patiently for it. When it arrives, you jump at it.

It is like a surfer. He doesn't create the waves. All he does is get ready, and wait for the waves. So you have to be prepared and be watchful for your divine opportunities.

Winners know that so-called 'luck' is the intersection of preparation and opportunity. If an individual is not prepared, he may not see or take advantage of an opportunity. Opportunities abound, but only those who are prepared utilise them effectively. When asked by a news reporter how she thought she would do in one of her early career swimming events in the United States several years ago, 14-year-old Australian Shane Gould replied, "I have a feeling there will be a world record today." She went on to set two world records in the one hundred and two hundred meter freestyle events. When asked how she thought she would fare in the more testing, grueling, four hundred meter event, Shane replied with a smile, "I get stronger every race, and besides ...

my parents said they'd take me to Disneyland if I win, and we're leaving tomorrow!" She went to Disneyland with three world records. At 16 she held five world records and became one of the greatest swimmers of all time, winning three gold medals in the 1972 Olympics.

She learned early about the power of self-expectancy.[iii]

> Winners appear to be fortunate because their positive expectancy enables them to be better prepared for their opportunities.

No opportunity comes to the un-expectant. If the opportunity comes, he may not recognize it. God is not going to ask someone to sow a car into your life if you don't have a driver's license. You have to show your desire by your readiness. Are you prepared for what God is about to do in your life? Preparation is a sign of expectation. For the Christian, the expectation is in sight.

> *"For surely there is an end; and thine expectation shall not be cut off"* (Proverbs 23:18, KJV).

One morning a man went out to start his car to go to Church. Flat tyre, no problem, he had a spare. He changed the tyre quickly and went on his way. He didn't think to drop the damaged tyre off to be fixed. "I'll get around to it," he said. Within five days he went to get the car to go to school. Another flat! Only this time no spare! He had to roll it to the nearest station and waited while it was fixed. When something breaks, fix it now. Don't wait until you need it and then you

> If you are going to make it i life, you have to take risks. Risk is what keeps a potential winner at bay and unprepared. Winners see risk as opportunity. They see the rewards of success in advance. They do not fear the penalties of failure.

don't have it! The man did not expect another puncture so he did not prepare.

Some people have had wonderful waves of opportunities and wasted them because they were scared to jump into the deep. Inadequate preparation can cause fear. Fear can cripple expectation and low expectation means inadequate preparation. It becomes a cycle. If you are going to make it in life, you have to take risks. Risk is what keeps a potential winner at bay and unprepared. Winners see risk as opportunity. They see the rewards of success in advance. They do not fear the penalties of failure. Those that succumb to fear become critics of those that do not. After they miss their opportunities, they start to criticise those who took advantage of theirs; those who have jumped into the sea of opportunities, making money, growing Churches, buying houses and making indelible marks. Fear can paralyse to the point where you submit to just getting-by. This attitude will never guarantee a good finish. For you to succeed in life, you need to doubt your doubts and replace your fear with faith.

The opportunity that is presented to you puts value on your time. Without opportunity, time is useless. For instance, if someone places a demand on your time without giving you advance notice, releasing that time for them will indicate how much value you place on your time.

Key Points to Remember

1. Take responsibility for your actions. What happened yesterday may not be your fault but what you become tomorrow will be your responsibility.

2. Spend your time wisely. What makes the difference between your making it in life or

otherwise is how you spend your time and take advantage of the opportunities that come your way.

3. Be ready for your opportunity; it may come anytime. Winners know that so-called luck is the intersection of preparation and opportunity. They appear to be fortunate because their positive self-expectancy enables them to better be prepared for their opportunities. Preparation is a sign of expectation.

4. If you are going to make it in life, you have to take risks. Inability to take risk is what keeps a potential winner at bay and unprepared. Winners see risk as opportunity. They see the rewards of success in advance. They do not fear the penalties of failure.

CHAPTER 2

God Knows Your Time

CHAPTER 2

God Knows Your Time

God knows the years He has apportioned for everyone and the number of years we are supposed to stay here on earth; we don't. He has it all written in His diary.

> *"For You formed my inward parts; you covered me in my mother's womb. I will praise You, for I am fearfully and wonderfully made; marvellous are Your works, and that my soul knows very well. My frame was not hidden from You, when I was made in secret, and skillfully wrought in the lowest parts of the earth. Your eyes saw my substance, being yet*

unformed. AND IN YOUR BOOK THEY ALL WERE WRITTEN, THE DAYS FASHIONED FOR ME, WHEN AS YET THERE WERE NONE OF THEM. How precious also are Your thoughts to me, O God! How great is the sum of them! If I should count them, they would be more in number than the sand; when I awake, I am still with You" (Psalms 139:13-18, Emphasis mine).

You came to earth as an answer to someone's request. Someone has a need so God fashioned you to meet that need and sent you to earth on a divine assignment. You are important to God. You are not a spectator; you are a major player in God's scheme of life. God then apportions the number of years you will require for the assignment to be completed and this is recorded in His book. In the same way, God knows exactly how long it will take me to fulfil His vision for my life on earth and so gives me all the years that are needed to do the task.

This is the good part of it: as long as you are in the will of God for your life, you cannot die before your years are completed and the job accomplished. The devil will try to weaken, discourage, or even attack you but you cannot die until your assignment is completed.

When you say you do not have time for something, it means one of three things:

1. You are trying to do what was never part of God's plan for you;
2. You have already wasted God's allocated time doing what was outside His will for you;
3. Or it is not His appointed time for that thing to be accomplished.

For instance, if I couldn't find time to write this book it would mean either of three things: God didn't ask me to write it so there was no time allocated for writing this book in His diary; I might have wasted my time doing other things He never intended for me to do; or the writing of the book is in the future.

God does not give everyone the same number of days or years; He gives sufficient time to get the job done. He allocates our days depending on our assignment. As in the physical, the time it will take for any job to be completed will depend on the nature of the job. Some may take many days and some few days or even years. Fulfilling the number of your days in God's reckoning is not as important as finishing the assignment and finishing well.

Master your time. It is the currency of the life. This is one of the things God gave everyone equally. People who are making impact have not been given more time than you. They have only maximised it in a way it can profit them. If you spend your time wisely you will finish well. Spend it foolishly and you have yourself to blame. Do the right thing at the right time and you will quickly notice the profit it will bring to you.

Master your time. It is the currency of the life. This is one of the things God gave everyone equally. People who are making impact have not been given more time than you.

There is time for everything

"To everything there is a season, a time for every purpose under heaven: a time to be born, and a time to die; a time to plant, and a time to pluck what is planted; a time to kill, and a time to heal; a time to break down, and a time to build up; a time to weep, and a time to laugh; a time to mourn, and a time to dance; a time to cast away stones, and a time to gather stones; a time to embrace, and a time to refrain from embracing; a time to gain, and a time to lose; a time to keep, and a time to throw away; a time to tear, and a time to sew; a time to keep silence, and a time to speak; a time to love, and a time to hate; a time of war, and a time of peace. What profit has the worker from that in which he labours? I have seen the God-given task with which the sons of men are to be occupied. He has made everything beautiful in its time. Also He has put eternity in their hearts, except that no one can find

out the work that God does from beginning to end. I know that nothing is better for them than to rejoice and to do good in their lives, and also that every man should eat and drink and enjoy the good of all his labour - it is the gift of God. I know that whatever God does, it shall be forever. Nothing can be added to it, and nothing taken from it. God does it that men should fear before Him. That which is has already been, and what is to be has already been; and God requires an account of what is past" (Ecclesiastes 3:1-15).

The Hebrew word translated time is the word 'et.' In its general use, it means a period of time, an appointed time, a proper time or season. 'Et' connotes time conceived as an opportunity or season as in a fixed, set time or period. It is also used secondarily of the concept of proper or appropriate time or suitable time as for the time God has appointed for one to die or carry out a given activity in life. A third use of the word connotes a season or a regular fixed period of time such as springtime, harvest time, time of life, rainy season, period of the day and so on.

In the Greek language there are three main divisions of time: chronos where we get chronology; kairos which means season; and hora which is translated hour. Time is an event while season is a series or periods of events. The hours of each day make up the seasons and the seasons make up our years. There are seasons of events within the time we are born and the time we die. The number of our days is a length of time while the events in our lives occur in seasons. The days measure the quantity while the season measures the quality. So Solomon begins the chapter of one of his books by saying everything has a purpose, a time and a season.

> *"To everything there is a season, a time for every purpose under heaven: a time to be born and a time to die"* (Ecclesiastes 3:1-2).

For every full measure of life there are three seasons: a morning season, an afternoon season and a night season, and each season is presented with lots of opportunities.

For every full measure of life there are three seasons: a morning season, an afternoon season and a night season, and each season is presented with lots of opportunities.

Key Points to Remember

1. Do your own bit. You are not on earth as a spectator. You are an answer to someone's question. God fashioned you to meet a need and sent you to earth on a divine assignment.

2. You are not going to live here forever. God knows the years He has apportioned for you and the number of days you are supposed to stay here on earth; you don't. So don't waste your time.

3. Plan to finish well. Fulfilling the number of your days in God's reckoning is not as important as finishing the assignment and finishing well.

CHAPTER 3

The Morning of Life

CHAPTER 3

The Morning of Life

Paul said,

"When I was a child, I spoke as a child, I understood as a child, I thought as a child; but when I became a man, I put away childish things" (I Corinthians 13:11).

How spot on that scripture is? Paul said that a child speaks first before he understands and then thinks. If you see someone who speaks before understanding or thinking, that person is like a child. But then Paul became 'a man.' You have to 'become' a man. Age is not an indicator of maturity. Some say that you mature with age. This may not always be true. People can be mentally retarded or physically less able though they are grown-ups. You are only a child once but can be forever immature. You do not suddenly begin to think unless you first become. It is a gradual but non-guaranteed process. You can be physically matured but be mentally retarded.

This is also true of Christians. There are countless number of people in Churches who are immature though saved for a long time. Their Church attendance record can be a hundred percent yet their spiritual temperature can be very low. They have full understanding of Church liturgy but a scanty Christian library. All their Christian lives, they have been feeding on milk and have refused to grow up. You'll find such people attend evening sessions at conferences instead of day sessions where they can study the word of God. They have made many preachers' pockets fat. Call a soul winning event, they will never come. Invite a motivational preacher and they'll call sick to work. Evening sessions where I had been motivational in my approach were always packed compared to the day teaching sessions. The only exception are those by the nature of their professions may not be given time off to attend morning meetings.

To grow up spiritually, you have to feed on real food, not milk. You have to 'become'. We all started life as babies but we cannot remain babies. The only two people that started life as grown-ups were Adam and Eve.

Jesus also was born as a baby in a manger. Then,

> *"Jesus grew up in wisdom and stature and in favour with God and all the people"* (Luke 2:52, NLT).

When Jesus became of age (12 years old), He made a decision to think no longer like a baby. He was assumed to have been following the relatives on their way back from an annual Passover festival but He was gone to Church.

"Three days later they finally discovered Him in the Temple, sitting among the religious teachers, listening to them and asking questions. All who heard Him were amazed at His understanding and His answers. His parents didn't know what to think. "Son," His mother said to Him, "why have You done this to us? Your father and I have been frantic, searching for you everywhere." "But why did you need to search?" He asked. "Didn't you know that I must be in my Father's house?" But they didn't understand what He meant. Then He returned to Nazareth with them and was obedient to them. And His mother stored all these things in her heart. Jesus grew in wisdom and in stature and in favour with God and all the people" (Luke 2:46-52, NLT).

Jesus was first spiritually matured before he was physically matured. He grew up first in wisdom before adding stature; *"Jesus grew up in wisdom and stature."*

Even His parents could not catch up with His level of understanding; *"But they didn't understand what he meant."* He questioned their lack of understanding when He asked *"Didn't you know I must be in My Father's house?"*

He also dazed the religious teachers with His level of understanding; *"All who heard Him were amazed at His understanding and His answers."*

All these happened before Jesus became a teenager. He then matched up His physical growth with spiritual maturity. He had to snatch Himself up from people's expectation. In other words, He 'became'. You do not have to remain a baby Christian; you too can 'become'.

To 'become' involves a deliberate definite decision. This stage before you 'become,' corresponds to the morning of life. It is the foundation stage where a lot of work needs to be done. Whatever happens, careful attention needs to be given and paid to this stage. The future of every person is shaped at this stage.

> *"If the foundation be destroyed, what can the righteous do?" (Psalms 11:3). Simpler renderings of this verse say: "The foundations of law and order have collapsed. What can the righteous do?" (Psalms 11:3, NLT); "There is nothing a good person can do when everything falls apart"* (Psalms 11:3, GNB).

If this stage of life is not carefully structured with God's guidance, a man may live the rest of his life trying to correct the past. Even the righteous (God-fearing, God-loving, prayerful man) will have a challenge. *"What can the righteous do?"* David asked.

This is a stage when a child is built-up. It is a life formation stage where the child learns to trust people, formulates a worldview, develops habits, struggles with life's meaning, develops their creativity, copes with demanding school work, peer pressure, has identity crises, speech and language formation, or struggles with sexuality. There is a lot going for them at this stage. So we are admonished to,

> *"Teach children how they should live, and they will remember it all their life"* (Proverbs 22:6, GNB).

This stage is also the dependence stage. A child at this stage depends on others for supply, support, strength, and safety - supply when in need; support in the pursuit of their aspirations; strength when weak; and safety when vulnerable. They lean on their parents, carers as well as guardians; on teachers as well as governments.

Sometimes parents and carers do a good job at bringing them up. Unfortunately, many do not. Because children are not allowed to choose for themselves, the onus is on us to make wise decisions on their behalf. It is rather unfortunate that the future of many have been destroyed by bad leadership of parents and carers. Many innocent children have become victims of bad governance, circumstances, and the environment in which they grew up. As a result of missed opportunities many people have been condemned to a life sentence of robbery, child labour, drug abuse, child prostitution, gun crimes, and abuse in many other forms, ranging from sexual to mental abuse and other mishaps due to no fault of their own.

"We missed him. Our chance to change things came and passed and we did not know it was there." A little boy sat through Sunday School classes for three years at a great Baptist Church (First Church, San Antonio) but someone missed him. His name was Sirhan Sirhan, and at age 24 he shot and killed Senator Robert Kennedy. In a welter of words and the shudder of grief throughout the nation, the persistent thought keeps recurring...someone missed him," said Dr. Jimmy Allen.[1]

The Bible puts this age group around birth to twenty or twenty-five years. By age twenty five people are treated as a fully grown, responsible adult. They are not expected to take major responsibilities before they turn twenty. There are twenty one Bible references instructing men to be enlisted for service when they reach twenty. Here are just a few of them.

> *"You and Aaron are to take a census of the people of Israel by clans and families. List the names of all the men twenty years old or older who are fit for military service'"* (Numbers 1:2-3, GNB).

> *"The LORD said to Moses, 'From the age of 25 each Levite shall perform the duties in the Tent of my presence, and at the age of 50 he shall retire. After that, he may help his fellow-Levites in performing their duties in the Tent, but he must not perform any service by himself. This is how you are to regulate the duties of the Levites'"* (Numbers 8:23-26, GNB).

The children of Israel are expected to pay offering as 'ransom money' when they reach twenty. They are not expected to pay this money before age twenty as their parents did that on their behalf. But at twenty they are expected to start working and be able to afford such offering. At twenty they also contributed to the building materials for the Tabernacle. That was expected because they could work.

> "*Everyone included among those who are numbered, from twenty years old and above, shall give an offering to the LORD"* (Exodus 30:14).
>
> *"A bekah for each man ([that is], half a shekel, according to the shekel of the sanctuary), for everyone included in the numbering from twenty years old and above, for six hundred and three thousand, five hundred and fifty [men]"* (Exodus 38:26).

The Israelites were also considered innocent before they turned twenty. God commanded those that were twenty years and older to be killed so they don't pollute the younger ones.

"The carcasses of you who have complained against Me shall fall in this wilderness, all of you who were numbered, according to your entire number, from twenty years old and above" (Numbers 14:29).

This is my point. According to the Bible any person below twenty is considered young. They are innocent and should not have to work. So the responsibility of their care lies with parents, guardians or government authorities. This is a big responsibility which should not be taken lightly. Today, the work age has been drastically widened, between 16 and 75 years.

"I have singled him (Abraham) out so that he will direct his sons and their families to keep the way of the LORD and do what is right and just" (Genesis 18:19, NLT).

"Teach your children to choose the right path, and when they are older, they will remain upon it. Just as the rich rule the poor, so the borrower is servant to the lender" (Proverbs 22:6-7, NLT).

"And now a word to you parents. Don't keep on scolding and nagging your children, making them angry and resentful. Rather, bring them up with the loving discipline the Lord Himself approves, with suggestions and godly advice" (Ephesians 6:4, TLB).

"Now I am coming to you again, the third time; and it is still not going to cost you anything, for I don't want your money. I want you! And anyway, you are my children, and little children don't pay for their father's and mother's food – it's the other way around; parents supply food for their children" (II Corinthians 12:14, TLB).

"Good people leave an inheritance to their grandchildren, but the sinner's wealth passes to the godly" (Proverbs 13:22, NLT).

The best we can do for our younger generation is not just to leave them money or wealth. What they need is for them to know God and be known by God.

When they have God, they will have money. Without leading them in the way of the Lord, they will waste the wealth we give them. If they are taught the way of the Lord, then they will be good stewards of God's resources. We have to get this priority right.

We can also bring up our children by commanding, directing, teaching, disciplining, training, providing and giving them godly advice. This is our duty of care and it is an enormous responsibility. We can best do this through modelling. What we do speaks volumes to them, more than what we say.

We can also get them the right education if we can afford to. If we do, we would have given them the right to choose. Remember, education gives people information but cannot make wise people. Education cannot make people successful but it provides them a choice. Let us work hard at getting them the right education so they can be free to go whichever way they choose without limitations.

We need also to help our children in channelling their energies creatively. We can help them to build good, lasting friendships and trust. As future leaders we need to help them to develop good morals, godly habits, issues of sex and sexuality, the meaning of life and right world views. We owe them this due diligence.

As soon as people slip out of this age group without good foundation, though they might have attained physiological maturity and physical independence, they can remain mentally bound by their past or upbringing. They resign themselves to what is called NFA (No Future Ambition) or choose to be wild, loose, and become a grade two NFA (No Fixed Address). Of course, without education and good skills, what else can they do? We do not want our children to end up as NEET (No Education, Employment or Training). We want them to be neat, clean, and valuable members of our quickly abating societies.

Maybe you are already feeling that your own life is being described and you think life has short-changed you. Do not despair, there is hope. Your past may not be your fault, but what you do with your future is entirely your choice. Your start may be bad but you can have a good finish.

It was 1818 in France. Louis, a boy of 9 years was sitting in his father's workshop. The father was a harness-maker and the boy loved to watch his father work the leather. "Someday father," said Louis, "I want to be a harness-maker, just like you."

"Why not start now?" said the father. He took a piece of leather and drew a design on it. "Now, my son," he said. "Take the hole-puncher and a hammer and follow this design, but be careful that you don't hit your hand."

Excited, the boy began to work, but when he hit the hole-puncher; it flew out of his hand and pierced his eye! He lost the sight of that eye immediately. Later, sight in the other eye failed. Louis was now totally blind.

A few years later, Louis was sitting in the family garden when a friend handed him a pine cone. As he ran his sensitive fingers over the cone, an idea came to him. He became enthusiastic and began to create an alphabet of raised dots on paper so that the blind could feel and interpret what was written. Thus, Louis Braille opened up a whole new world for the blind – all because of an accident![ii]

Louis was an accident victim who refused to condemn himself and be a burden on his carers. He decided to change his life and those of many like him. He had a bad experience but a good finish.

My late dad is another good example. He came from a family that was poor. His father was a peasant farmer and so was his mother. They could not afford to pay for his education.

At an early age, he sacrificed his education for work. From his meagre wages he managed to send his siblings to school one by one. Dad also saved up to take care of his father and pay for private tuition for himself up to his first degree.

Dad pursued his teaching career to the point of becoming the Vice-Principal of a college and shortly before his appointment as the Principal of another college he was invited to serve the state government in a bigger capacity.

From grass to grace! That is what best describes him. He went from zero to become a hero. He was appointed a State Commissioner by two successive political governments during two different regimes. Dad travelled the world, used the best cars, and lived in fantastic accommodations.

As a godly man, he was appointed the head chief of the Chieftaincy Council in his hometown, a post which remained empty four years after his demise. He sponsored all his children up to university and my mum didn't have to work after she was 45. Dad died in service at the age of 69 and received a State burial in recognition of his contribution to the welfare and development of the State. The ceremony took place at the largest city Cathedral covered by the local and national media. He was buried in style. He was born a pauper, but buried a prince.

> Do not allow your past to become the obstacle against your future. Forget what could have been and focus on the present and the future.

My dad did not condemn himself. You should not. He could have spent his entire life building blame bricks on his parents who though tried their best, could not help their son. He just tried to make the best out of the rest of his humble existence and his efforts were very well rewarded.

As a child of God, there is no technical knock-out in this battle. You can still get up and be somebody in life. Let's just suppose your morning was rough; your parents really tried to educate you but couldn't make ends meet. You even tried to help yourself but it proved too difficult. Do not allow your past to become the obstacle against your future. Forget what could have been and focus on the present and the future.

> *"No, dear brothers, I am still not all I should be but I am bringing all my energies to bear on this one thing: FORGETTING THE PAST AND LOOKING FORWARD TO WHAT LIES AHEAD"* (Philippians 3:13, TLB Emphasis mine).

> *"Make good use of every opportunity you have, because these are evil days"* (Ephesians 5:18, GNB).

You don't have to condemn yourself to a life sentence of lack or failure. You may not be able to recover the past but you can redeem the future. Welcome to your afternoon!

Key Points to Remember

1. As parents and carers, the best we can do for our younger generation is not just to leave them money or wealth. What they need most is to know God and be known by God. If they are taught the way of the Lord, they will be good stewards of God's resources.

2. Sit with your children and discuss issues of sex and sexuality, the meaning of life and right world views. You owe them this due diligence.

3. If you are a young adult and you feel crushed, don't give up; there is no knock-out in this battle. Your beginning may be rough; you can still get up and be somebody in life. Do not allow your past to become the obstacles against your future. Forget what could have been and focus on the present and the future.

i. Dr. Jimmy Allen, former pastor of First Baptist Church, San Antonio, Texas in Pulpit Helps, May, 1991.

ii. Bits and Pieces, June, 1990, pp. 23-24.

CHAPTER 4

The Afternoon of Life

CHAPTER 4

The Afternoon of Life

The morning of life is the laying of foundations while the afternoon of life is the building stage. It is the time for building a home, not an edifice. Building a house is important but secondary to building a home. It is the stage where to get married and start having children. It is also a stage of building a career, a profession and then buying houses. This is the stage when things begin to solidify and set in stones. What people do at this stage in life will stay with them for the rest of their life.

The people in this age group sustain the airlines.

They are the ones going around the world shopping for business. This age group keeps the economy buoyant. If you pull them out of employment, the economy of any nation, no matter how strong, will collapse. They are the largest group in employment.

This group also sustains the housing market. When someone get past this age group, they may have to deposit twice or sometimes more as down-payment for a property as a first time buyer.

> *"We admire the strength of youth and respect the grey hair of age"* (Proverbs 20:29, GNB).

Young people have a lot of strength but for many of them unfortunately, what should have been an asset is deployed on unprofitable ventures now working against them. Rather than utilise their privileged positions and God-given resources to procure their future, youths tend to see their energy as something that will never diminish. They forget that time is God-given and opportunities are divinely orchestrated.

Wasted opportunity means wasted time and more wasted opportunities and time. The cycle is never ending.

With a lot of energy and money, these 'city boys' (as they are sometimes described) travel the world partying and engaging in all forms of activities of temporal value. Instead of securing a future for themselves and their families, they squander, misuse and sometimes abuse their opportunities. They dissipate their energy and fritter away their future.

Time is God given and opportunities are divinely orchestrated. Wasted opportunity means wasted time and more wasted opportunities and time. The cycle is never ending.

They call it enjoyment. Others call it youthful exuberance. It is misplaced priorities and a waste of time. Something within says to them: "You are still young, if you don't enjoy now, you can't enjoy when you are older. Don't let any man (or woman) lock you in the prison of marriage, enjoy your life" (as if being married is bondage). “If you have children now, you won’t be able to enjoy freedom anymore.” “Why buy a house now, you are only twenty five; why not wait? You won’t have money anymore to spare. Without disposable income, you won’t be able to afford nice things just like your peers.”

None of the above is true. Marriage is not bondage. Though it is fraught with many challenges, it is still the first and best institution God created. Despite the rising divorce statistics, many unmarried people want to get married and widows, widowers and divorcees rush to remarry. What is responsible for this? I do not know. But I think the idea is that being married is good. I am not suggesting that you should rush into marriage but there are a lot of benefits and advantages if you marry early.

It is equally untrue that having children early takes away your freedom or liberty. It may appear to be so at the beginning, but it is rewarding and fulfilling all the same. The joy you have when the children grow up and are semi-independent or independent is immeasurable. If they do well in life, the parents are thrilled and show them off to their friends. It even sounds selfish to consider any child as a burden on the parents. You should dispense your energies on your children than on anything else. At the end of the day, your family will be all you have left. Same can be said of owning your own home while you are still young.

"Enjoy a little, travel a little, and put your tomorrow on pause?" If all you do is squander the financial resources God gives you, you may have been deceived. For Jesus said,

> *"We must work the works of Him who sent Me and be busy with His business while it is daylight; night is coming on, when no man can work"* (John 9:4, AMP).

Moses also echoed the same sentiment when he said,

"Seventy years are given us! And some may even live to eighty. But even the best of these years are often emptiness and pain; soon they disappear, and we are gone. Teach us to number our days and recognise how few they are; help us to spend them as we should" (Psalms 90:10, 12, TBN).

Moses said we are to live for 70 and possibly 80, but they are nothing. '*So Lord teach us to number* (not count) *our days*'. Why? In order "That we may apply wisdom." When we celebrate our birthdays, we count the length of our days. But Moses did not ask us to count the length of our days, he asked us to number them. When we number our days, it gives us an idea of how they have been spent and how far away from 80 we are. Counting our days is about quantity while numbering our days is about quality.

Some people live while others exist. If we are to live rather than just exist, it starts with being in the centre of God's will for our lives and if by 70 or 80 we could not find fulfilment, then we have just existed. So God gives to each of us a specific number of days or years to live. Though we count our years in upward increments, we really should be counting down. As we grow in years, we get physically older. We start to die from the day we make our earthly entry. So Moses said *"…so we can apply wisdom."* Wisdom is what we need to live right.

> In life, we don't often get one opportunity twice. We always think we have more than one 'chance.' No, it is not true.

In life, we don't often get one opportunity twice. We always think we have more than one 'chance.' No, it is not true. We may have another chance or another opportunity to do what should have been done before. It is always another chance, never the same one twice. To have the same opportunity, we would need to rewind time or God may have to extend our days to accommodate the lost time or reschedule our assignment. I mean, cut down our earthly assignment.

Having a second or third chance is not even the norm, it is an exception. So don't miss your opportunities. That may prove expensive. Don't squander it. Seize the moment and maximise the opportunities. If you believe the devil that says 'you still have your whole life ahead of you,' you might have sold your birthright and future to him just as Esau did to Jacob.

If you buy now and postpone the payment, you may pay more dearly and direly for it in the future. You can choose to enjoy life now and pay for it later or you can choose to sacrifice your pleasures and comforts at this time so you can enjoy later. This is called delayed or deferred gratification. It is possible to have a good start but end woefully. However, it is better to have a good start and have a good finish. Your better can become bad if it prevents you from your best. What you call your present 'best' can be 'bettered'. There is so much more ahead of you. Don't even settle for the best – reach higher, there is always more ahead.

Just Imagine

1. A twenty five year mortgage paid off; your last child graduating from the university when you are 50; and retiring from actively running your own business as you have been doing for the last twenty five years.

2. You don't have to go to work because of a mortgage at age 50. You stop changing nappies at 32 years of age. Or you have control over your time as a company director at twenty five years of age.

3. Sitting on a 500% returns by the age of 50, or leaving home without having to worry about baby sitters when you are 40, or re-setting your own salary every year if you so wish.

Did you notice the figures 25 and 50? That's right. I have done that deliberately to say this,

"The LORD said to Moses, 'From the age of 25 each Levite shall perform the duties in the Tent of

my presence, and at the age of 50 he shall retire. After that, he may help his fellow-Levites in performing their duties in the Tent, but he must not perform any service by himself. This is how you are to regulate the duties of the Levites'" (Numbers 8:23-26, GNB).

You could say that Bill Gates fulfilled this scripture, retiring as the CEO of Microsoft at an early age to focus on things more dear to his heart. At the age of 50, we should retire from active labour. So says the Bible. We are from then supposed to participate in supportive roles. But if the divinely allocated time and opportunities have been missed, you may have to work longer and harder to make ends meet. When will you then have time for God?

This worried David so much that he inquired of God to tell him how many days have been allocated to him to live on earth.

"Please, LORD, show me my future. Will I soon be gone? You made my life short, so brief that the time means nothing to you. Human life is but a breath, and it disappears like a shadow. Our struggles are senseless; we store up more and more, without ever knowing who will get it all" (Psalms 39:4-6, CEV).

GRABBED OR MISSED OPPORTUNITIES

I became a Church leader within a year and a half of joining my fellowship. I started attending a new believers' class called BBC (Believers' Bible Class) straightaway. I joined the class as a student although I had been born again ten years before but had never been through a structured teaching on the basics of the new birth.

After the session which lasted 3 months, I was invited by our teacher to assist him during the next class session. I had thought I would be an usher helping to make the class conducive for studies. I soon realised it was in a teaching capacity after he asked me to prepare to do lecture him on one of the curriculum subjects at his house.

He was so impressed by my presentation that after he introduced me as his new assistant, he never came back to the class. Not that he left the Church; he just took a risk at trusting God, my teaching gift, and skill. From then on I became our Church's BBC teacher. Within months, I also launched the BBC course at other branches and became the National BBC Coordinator.

It was my opportunity. I saw it and grabbed it. As soon as I was asked by my teacher to make the presentation, I did not fret or refuse the offer. Not that I had done it before in that capacity but I was willing to give it my all. (Of course I was a teacher and a tutor before relocating to England). I fasted and prayed. Then I studied the subject until I almost became an authority on it. I researched as if it was a thesis. I bought books and revised hard just on this one subject.

Why did I go to that length? It was my opportunity and I did not want to miss it. From then on, my promotion was rapid – from a non-stipendiary BBC teacher to the full-time denomination's Bible College Provost, in just five years. My quest and thirst for God led me to a further study at a Bible College in the UK. I do not yet know as I should but I keep learning and finding out. Whatever God achieved with me, He can with you.

One day many years ago a bright boy found employment in a photograph gallery in Nashville, Tennessee. His wages were small, but he took good care of them, and in the course of time he had saved up a snug little sum of money. One day a friend less thrifty than he came to him with a long face, and asked for a loan of money, offering a book as security. Although the other knew there was little probability of his ever being repaid, he could not refuse the request. 'Here is the money; keep your book and repay me when you can.'

The grateful lad went away in such haste that he left the book behind. The kind youth examined the volume with curiosity. It was a work on astronomy, by Dick, and it so fascinated him that he sat up all night studying it. He had never read anything which so filled him with delight. He determined to learn all that he could about the wonders of the heavens. He began thenceforth to read everything he could obtain relating to astronomy.

The next step was to buy a small spy-glass, and night after night he spent most of the hours on the roof of his house studying the stars. He secured, second hand, the tube of a larger spy-glass, into which he fitted an eye-piece, and sent to Philadelphia for an object glass. By and by he obtained a five-inch (130mm) glass retractor telescope, which, as you know, is an instrument of considerable size.

Meanwhile he worked faithfully in the shop of the photographer; but his nights brought him rare delight, for he was never tired of tracing out the wonders and marvels of the worlds around us. With the aid of his large spy-glass he discovered two comets before they were seen by any of the professional astronomers, whose superior instruments were continually scanning the heavens in search of the celestial wanderers. This exploit, you may well suppose, made the boy famous. He was invited by the professors in Vanderbilt University to go thither and see what he could do with their six-inch telescope. He never graduated from the school, but he did receive the only honorary degree Vanderbilt had ever awarded. In the course of the following four years he discovered six comets. He was next engaged by the Lick Observatory. With the aid of its magnificent instrument he discovered eight comets, and astonished the world by discovering the fifth satellite of Jupiter, Amalthea. He invented a new method of photographing the nebulae in the Milky Way, and has shown an originality approaching genius in his work in star photography.

Perhaps you have already guessed the name of this famous astronomer, which is Prof. Edward Emerson Barnard in charge of the Yerkes Observatory of Chicago University, and this is the story of how he worked up.[i] If you are ever going to climb the ladder of finishing well where only few dare to, you need to keep learning and remain focused on the object.

In 1991 Thomas Dexter, a country preacher met with Sarah Jordan Powell (the noted gospel singer known as the songbird of the Church of God in Christ) at a small dinner conference. The meeting provided Dexter the long awaited opportunity to invite this national Fine Arts Director of the second largest Pentecostal denomination in the world (who also happened to be a well-travelled gospel singer with eight albums to her credit) to minister in song in one of his services while he preached. The trip to West Virginia provided an opportunity for Powell to marvel at the preaching of Dexter.

Like most black preachers nationwide, Dexter knew about the Azusa Conference held yearly in April and was impressed by the fact that his new ally was a close friend of the host. A year after Powell visited his Church, Dexter called to inform her of his plan to attend the next Conference. After the evening session of the second day Dexter finally realised his ambition to meet the Conference host having been introduced by his new acquaintance. At the meeting, a taped message of one of Dexter's meetings was forced into the hands of the Conference host.

After listening to the tape and with a little persuasion from Powell, Dexter was invited by Carlton Pearson later in the year to keynote mini-Azusa, a regional meeting of ministerial leaders of the Azusa fellowship held at Higher Dimensions, Pearson's home church alongside two other ministers, Mark Hanby and Brian Keith Williams. Pearson decided to play segments of Hanby, Williams and Dexter's sermons preached at the ministerial leaders' meeting on his television program, and his production staff took great care to edit them down to seven-minute clips portraying each preacher at his best.

A seven-minute clip from an hour long message titled 'Behind Closed Doors' was only a third of a day slot on a TV airing contract Pearson had with a Christian broadcasting network. By sheer coincidence (or rather, God-incidence), the President and founder of the network happened to tune to his own network after a tiring day of intense contemplation. It was at this time the programme was being aired – at the very minute the best seven minutes of the message was being aired.

As it happened, Paul Crouch, the founder of Trinity Broadcasting Network (TBN) was writing his autobiography 'I had no Father but God' at the time. Answers to some of the questions he was asking came listening to Thomas Dexter Jakes speak on this fateful day. Paul immediately inquired about this unknown guest preacher, requested the entire message, and aired it full length every Friday for the next eight weeks.

In February of the following year, Pearson invited T.D. Jakes back to Higher Dimensions - this time on a Sunday. Jakes preached his now classic sermon, 'The Puppet Master,' delineating how God works behind the scenes for believers in a manner resembling a puppet master pulling strings. A few weeks later, Pearson decided to call Jakes to invite him to speak at the main event, the Azusa Conference in April. After his experience with Paul Crouch playing his message on TBN, Jakes was no longer naïve about what television exposure could do for his career. He knew that many Azusa services were aired live on TBN, and since he had previously impressed Crouch, another classic sermon could produce tremendous momentum for his budding fame.

What do you preach to make a profound impact

at Azusa 93? Well, Jakes decided to preach 'Woman, Thou Art Loosed,' a sermon that was sparked by his successful Sunday school lessons back in West Virginia. The auditorium was jam-packed on the closing night of the conference. Pearson had to tell the workers to pull down the curtains to make more seats available to the waiting audience as they were beginning to be turned away. As a result 12,000 people came in that night to hear Jakes. That simply was it. The rest as they say is history. That was a grabbed opportunity; just one woman, Sarah Jordan Powell, and the expectant Jakes.[ii]

Don't miss your opportunity. This is the time. This is the moment. It is the time to serve God and serve Him wholeheartedly. This is the time to make money, and lots of it. Save a lot and invest or start your own business. It is the time to build or buy your house. It is the time to marry and start a family, have all your seven children quickly.

It reminds me of the story of two salesmen sent to a country with a few shoes. On arrival they discovered that nobody wore shoes. It meant their few stocks were already too many. One of them called to his company to come and get him out of the country but the other requested for more stock. Their reason was the same, "No one wears shoes here." One of them saw obstacles and impossibilities but the other saw opportunities and possibilities.

Many people see big challenges and run away from what can be the big opportunities of a lifetime. They see problems and obstacles in every opportunity but winners and successful people see opportunities in every problem.

The army of Israel saw Goliath as an obstacle but David saw him as his opportunity to demonstrate God's awesome power and he eventually became the undisputed monarch in Israel. They saw the Philistine as being too big to hit, but David saw him as too big to miss. That was his opportunity.

In like manner, the ten spies saw the Philistine giants as unbeatable but the two spies Joshua and Caleb saw them as too small for their Jehovah God. They were the only two spies who made it to the Promised Land.

> Opportunities are missed because we look at the enormity of our challenges rather than the bigness of our God.

Many times we miss our opportunities because we look at the enormity of our challenge rather than the bigness of our God.

Some years ago an energetic young man began work as a clerk in a hardware store. Like many old time hardware stores, the inventory included thousands of dollars' worth of items that were obsolete or seldom called for by customers. The young man was smart enough to know that no thriving business could carry such an inventory and still show a healthy profit. He proposed a sale to get rid of the stuff. The owner was reluctant but finally agreed to let him set up a table in the middle of the store and try to sell off a few of the oldest items. Every product was priced at ten cents. The sale was a success and the young fellow got permission to run a second sale. It, too, went over just as well as the first.

This gave the young clerk an idea. Why not open a store that would sell only nickel and dime items? He could run the store and his boss could supply the capital. The young man's boss was not enthusiastic. "The plan will never work," he said, "because you can't find enough items to sell at a nickel and a dime." The young man was disappointed but eventually went ahead on his own and made a fortune out of the idea. His name was Frank Winfield Woolworth.

Years later his old boss lamented, "As near as I can figure it, every word I used in turning Woolworth down has cost me about a million dollars!"[iii]

If you are an employee reading this book, go back to work tomorrow and ask your boss to throw challenges your way. It may lead you to the discovery of your life – something you may never realise were it not for the challenge. If you are given an unusual task like tidying the kitchenette, don't just tidy it up; get a towel and gloves, and clean it up as if it were your house and your real paid job. Perhaps someone will notice the difference and give in a good word to your employer for you. Don't say you cannot do the job because it's beneath you.

If you are a potential employee required to make a ten minute presentation at an interview, do it as if it was a major international seminar. Give it all your best, study, research and get help to prepare your slides. That may be your opportunity.

If you serve in a Church and your pastor gives you a responsibility, don't say it belongs to a different department. Of course, your pastor knows. It's your opportunity to shine; just do it. If nobody else notices you, God does and will reward your willingness and humility.

Jacob was not preparing the red stew for Esau. He was preparing it for himself but he made it palatable enough for someone else to desire it. Don't do things shabbily either because it's yours or because it's not yours. Someone might be watching and take interest. When Esau asked for the stew, Jacob had his opportunity and grabbed it. He was ready. If he was not ready, he could have missed the birthright outright.

Minimise the Movement

Grab the moment. God brings the opportunity; all you need to do is get ready to grab it. Who knows when it will come? Don't mess around; use your energy wisely to your advantage. Stay focused on your career, job or profession. Don't jump from one job to another every six months. It's the time, it's the moment, don't let it slip by. You are not going to remain the same forever. Vigour diminishes; strength wanes; so use yours to the maximum. When you take hold of the moment, you take hold of the future. If you mishandle today, it may affect your tomorrow. Today was yesterday's tomorrow and your tomorrow will soon become today. Time waits for no man, so grab the moment. Minimise the movement, maximise the moment.

> Today was yesterday's tomorrow and your tomorrow will soon become today. If you mishandle today, it may affect your tomorrow.

"Even those who are young grow weak; young people can fall exhausted. But those who trust in the LORD for help will find their strength renewed. They will rise on wings like eagles; they will run and not get weary; they will walk and not grow weak" (Isaiah 40:30-31, GNB).

Key Points to Remember

1. Start early. If you are of a marrying age, do not rush into marriage but consider marrying early. If you can afford to, buy your own

house early. If you have a knack for business, start early too. Obtain your financial independence very early.

2. If you work, take regular but sensible breaks. Do not waste your resources and time; all the time being watchful for your own divine opportunities.

3. Life involves risks at all levels. Take risks. There are no safe risks. A risk is what it is called - a risk. Not taking risk is a bigger risk.

4. Do not be afraid of challenges. The more challenging the task, the more rewarding.

i. From "Present Day Parables" by J. Wilbur Chapman.

ii. Lee Shayne, TD Jakes: America's New Preacher (New York: New York University Press, 2005), pp. 33-60.

iii. Bits and Pieces, Vol. F, #41.

CHAPTER 5

The Evening of Life

CHAPTER 5

The Evening of Life

The evening of life is the consolidation stage when previous work and labour starts yielding interest. No mortgage to pay and less stress to face. This is when an individual becomes his own boss. It is a time all the children should have graduated from University or college. Some of the children may even be married. As to leisure, the evening of life is a time to travel around the world and enjoy the views.

Unfortunately, this is also the time of diminished vigour. Gradually failing health may mean that some things may become a struggle. Things that used to be straightforward and easy when someone is younger can become very tasking and daunting. Running up the stairs, running after buses, and jumping around with grandchildren, are a few of them.

One more thing; a person in the evening of life may be less employable. He may not be able to compete with twenty five year olds for a number of jobs except where many years of experience are required.

The question I get asked by many people at this stage of resting is this: "If my afternoon season was horrible, what do I do with my life now that I am old and aged?"

If you are in this age group, do not think you are condemned. It is not my intention to do so. I just want to challenge the youth enough so as to prevent them from wasting their lives but make the best of their God-given potentials and maximise this season.

Now to the answer: no life is useless. Someone

once said that age is in the mind. You are only as old as you think. I have seen many people of age achieved more than the younger ones. Abraham was called to a life of absolute devotion to God when he was 75. Another example is Moses who started his ministry when he was 80. And one of his disciples, Caleb took on a new project when he was 85.

> *"...Look at me! I am eighty-five years old and am just as strong today as I was when Moses sent me out. I am still strong enough for war or for anything else"* (Joshua 14:10-11, GNB).

Let us take a look at older people. It is generally believed that older people exist only to enjoy their old age. It sounds like they are whiling away the time waiting for the day of their death. Yes, they do enjoy the fruits of their labour, but they have not necessarily finished their assignment on planet earth. When Jesus finished His assignment, He was crucified. When Paul finished his assignment, he was killed.

You are not sustained on earth to kill time. In God's plan, old people are kept on earth to produce more fruit. When an old person ceases to be fruitful they will be called home. Fruit bearing for the righteous continues until death. Bible retirement is from active administrative responsibilities, not from ministry.

> *"They shall still bear fruit in old age; they shall be fresh and flourishing"* (Psalms 92:14).

You think the time is gone? No. There are many good things about being old. Most people will get old if Jesus tarries anyway. Rather than be afraid to grow old, you should begin to plan for that time.

> There is more in you than you think; a lot more that can still benefit millions. Don't die with them. You were loaded with gifts when you were born.

The richest place on earth is not a geographical location somewhere. It is at the back yard. It is at the graveyard where billions are buried with their gifts and talents. It's such a sad waste. There is more in you than you think; a lot more that can still benefit millions. Don't die with them. You were loaded with gifts when you were born. Your gifts are for people here on earth. You should not go to the grave with anything God purposed for the benefit of others. You should not die full but empty. Empty yourself. The more you do for God, the better your end.

The last assignment my dad had with the state government started when he was 65 years old. Not that there were no younger and more agile aspirants; he just had the experience required for the post. He did not even vie for it; he was appointed. The government discovered something in him and demanded it.

Even if it appears that the degeneration of the physical body is taking its toll on you, it should not be a reason or excuse to stop being active in the things of God. While you engage in the less physical side of living, you are very valuable in ministry to younger minds. Use the little strength left in you to serve the One who created you until He says it is time to quit.

> *"Be watchful, and strengthen the things which remain…"* (Revelation 3:2).

God is in the business of restoration and redemption. When we think about restoration, we always think in terms of physical things alone. On the other hand when we think about redemption, we often think in terms of spiritual things. Neither is the complete truth. God can restore physical as well as spiritual losses. In a similar manner, He can redeem losses in the spiritual and material. Do not worry about the years you've lost and how hopeless your situation may seem; God can and will redeem and restore them back to you. Your latter rain and the former rain can fall in the same month.

> *"See then that you walk circumspectly, not as fools but as wise, redeeming the time, because the days are evil"* (Ephesians 5:15).

> *"So I will restore to you the years that the swarming locust has eaten, the crawling locust, the*

consuming locust, and the chewing locust, My great army which I sent among you" (Joel 2:25).

One of the many good things about getting old is that you have a lot of experience on your side. This is also known as life's school.

"The glory of young men is their strength; of old men, their experience" (Proverbs 20:29, TBL).

Experience (good or bad) is one of the reasons we need older people around. We can learn from either. We can also learn from personal experiences. I once heard it said that 'only a fool doesn't learn from his own experience.'

A story is told of a young man by name Rehoboam who sought the advice of the elders who stood before his father Solomon while he was yet king. Rehoboam asked, "How do you advise me to answer these people?" The whole assembly of Israel had gone to ask Rehoboam to lighten their yoke. After asking the elders, Rehoboam also inquired of the young men on the same issue. They gave opposing advice to that of the elders.

Rehoboam rejected the advice of the elders but embraced that of the young men. Rather than relieve them, he added to the people's yoke. And that was the beginning of his end. Listen to what the people said to Rehoboam;

> *"What share do we have in David, what part in Jesse's son? To your tents, O Israel! Look after your own house, O David! So the Israelites went home"* (I Kings 12:16, NIV).

For ignoring the wisdom of the aged, the Israelite dynasty became divided during the reign of Rehoboam as foretold by prophet Ahijah the Shilonite. The entire story is told in I Kings, chapters 12 and 13.

The saying holds true that "Though the young may outnumber the aged on new clothes, never can the aged be outnumbered on old ones." When the young falls, he looks forward, but the aged look backwards.

Older people look to see what made them fall and learn from it but if you look forward when you fall, you probably will fall again on the same issue because you haven't looked for the reason why you fell. That is what is called experience. When we move close to the elderly, they can help us with their experience of the past for our future.

Older people have lots of understanding too. From the experience they have acquired through the years, understanding has been developed. Understanding is a sign of maturity. It distinguishes boys from men, children from adults, and young from elderly.

> *"Dear brothers and sisters don't be childish in your understanding of these things. Be innocent as babies when it comes to evil, but be mature and wise in understanding matters of this kind"* (I Corinthians 14:20, NLT).
>
> The NKJV puts the same scripture this way,
>
> *"... but in understanding be men"*

Having understanding is just as important as pursuing after wisdom. You cannot get wisdom without first having understanding. Solomon did not only pray for wisdom, he prayed for understanding as well. With understanding, God granted him wisdom, riches, honour and length of days.

> *"... Therefore give to Your servant an understanding heart to judge your people...Then God said to him, 'Because you ... have asked for yourself understanding to discern justice, ... I have given you a wise and understanding heart, ... riches and honour'"* (I Kings 3:1-14).

Wisdom without understanding is a dangerous weapon in the hands of a youth. Solomon was given wisdom and understanding, but he promoted wisdom and underplayed understanding.

Wisdom without understanding is a dangerous weapon in the hands of a youth. Solomon was given wisdom and understanding, but he promoted wisdom and underplayed understanding.

With his wisdom Solomon ended up with 300 wives and 700 concubines. He lost understanding and made many mistakes which cost him the kingdom – though not in his own lifetime. Therefore the Bible enjoins us not only to pursue wisdom, but also to get understanding – which is what aged people have.

> *"Wisdom is the principal thing, therefore get wisdom. And in all your getting, get understanding"* (Proverbs 4:7).

Get close to the elderly and draw understanding from them. Having understanding will give you better life.

> *"Understanding is a wellspring of life to him who has it. But the correction of fools is folly"* (Proverbs 16:22).

GLOSSARY OF UNDERSTANDING FROM THE BOOK OF PROVERBS

> *"A wise man will hear and increase learning, and a man of understanding will attain wise counsel"* (Proverbs 1:5).

"Discretion will preserve you; understanding will keep you" (Proverbs 2:11).

"Happy is the man who finds wisdom, and the man who gains understanding" (Proverbs 3:13).

"Hear, my children, the instruction of a father, and give attention to know understanding" (Proverbs 4:1).

"Say to wisdom, 'You are my sister, and call understanding your nearest kin" (Proverbs 7:4).

"Wisdom is found on the lips of him who has understanding, but a rod is for the back of him who is devoid of understanding" (Proverbs 10:13).

"Good understanding gains favour, but the way of the unfaithful is hard" (Proverbs 13:15).

"Wisdom rests in the heart of him who has understanding, but what is in the heart of fools is made known" (Proverbs 14:33).

"He who has knowledge spares his word, and a man of understanding is of a calm spirit. Even a fool is counted wise when he holds his peace; when

he shuts his lips, he is considered perceptive" (Proverbs 17:27-28).

"Counsel in the heart of a man is like deep water, but a man of understanding will draw it out" (Proverbs 20:5).

"A man who wanders from the way of understanding will rest in the assembly of the dead" (Proverbs 21:16).

Key Points to Remember

1. You are never too old to work for God. Though you may not take on physically demanding roles, consider a few ministry functions. Use the little strength left in you to serve the One who created you until He says it is time to quit.

2. Find willing and teachable young minds to mentor. Your experiences and understanding acquired over the years are gems for life. This

will be your new ministry. You can start a Caleb Ministry amongst your peers.

CHAPTER 6

Now Is Your Time

CHAPTER 6

Now Is Your Time

What we spend time on is an indication of where our priorities lie. We live in a world where priorities have been misplaced. People are their own gods. Most people are self-centred and selfish and lack any respect for authority or other people. Knowing and placing a value on certain priorities in life will help to determine how to manage and maximise your time. Your friends and family members want some of your time too. Setting priorities will help to allocate the time of the day in such a way that it can be maximised. Let me share with you how to manage your time based on biblical priorities.

Put God First

Priority number one is assigned to God Almighty. In all you do, acknowledging God is of utmost importance. No one can have a good finish without God's backing. If we take a look at the Ten Commandments you will notice that the first four commandments concern our relationship with God. They are found in Exodus 20:1-11 and Deuteronomy 5:6-15.

1. *You shall have no other gods before me.*
2. *You shall not make for yourself an idol.*
3. *You shall not misuse the name of the Lord your God.*
4. *Observe the Sabbath day by keeping it holy.*

Many people wrap God around their little fingers. They say things like 'If I am not at work and I have time, I will go to Church.' They ought to say 'if I don't have Church, I'll do this and that.' This is not to say that we should not work. It means we only do that which is required and before we agree to an extra shift or overtime. We must first establish what carries a greater priority: more work or God.

Time with God should be foremost and non-negotiable. This includes time to pray, time to study God's word, fellowship with brethren and attending Church. If God is more important, then He must be first. The Bible says we should seek God's kingdom first.

> *"But seek first the kingdom of God and His righteousness, and all these things shall be added to you"* (Matthew 6:33).

Jesus demonstrated this when He challenged His parents about their knowledge of His mission.

> *"'Why were you searching for Me?' He asked. 'DON'T YOU KNOW I had to be in My Father's house?' But they did not understand what He was saying to them"* (Luke 2:49-50, NIV).

No twelve-year old dares challenge their parents that way now! Jesus was telling His earthly father that there was a Higher Father. Now, if I were Joseph, that would have upset me. It's like a son telling his step dad that someone is more important than him. Yet He was not being rude. He was just stating a fact that should have been obvious - God is number One - a Creator far more important than His creation.

Later, Jesus also turned to His brothers and sisters. This is what He said,

> *"'Who are My mother and My brothers?' He asked. Then He looked at those seated in a circle around Him and said, 'Here are My mother and My brothers! Whoever does God's will is My brother and sister and mother'"* (Mark 3:33-35, NIV).

What a shock! His family must have either thought He had gone out of Himself or admit He knew what He was doing.

As if that was not enough, Jesus also turned to His disciples and said,

> *"If you want to be My follower you must love Me more than your own father and mother, wife and children, brothers and sisters - yes, more than your own life. Otherwise, you cannot be My disciple"* (Luke 14:26, NLT).

The point is this. In all His dealings, Jesus showed there was none more important than God, the Heavenly Father. He is Number One. I must admit, putting Him first in my life hasn't come easy. It is a daily crucifying of the flesh. It may demand going on missions when you'd rather go to Miami on holiday; reading your Bible when you'd rather read a novel; praying when you'd rather talk to friends; fasting when you'd rather feast. Putting God first means there are places we cannot go, things we cannot say, things we cannot look at, and saying sorry even when you've

There is none more important than God. He is Number One. I must admit, putting Him first in my life hasn't come easy.

been wronged. It means we have to put our desires secondary to God's will. Now you say that is not easy? No, it is not, but this we must do if we are to put God first.

YOU ARE NEXT

You come next. This is a difficult one for most humble believers to accept. The Bible does not teach that we should put other people first. No one can do that; otherwise he would be a hypocrite. Airlines tell us to first look after ourselves in the unlikely event of an emergency. The reason is that I will be of no value to anyone if I am of no good to myself. How can I help other people unless I have been helped? Whenever we find people taking this position, we make them feel guilty unnecessarily. We call them names: selfish, self-centred, and egocentric because they won't give to us. However, the fifth of the Ten Commandment is centred on our welfare. Let us read it in the Old and New Testaments.

"Honour your father and your mother. Then YOU will live a long, full life in the land the LORD your God will give YOU" (Exodus 20:12, NLT).

"Honour your father and mother – which is the first commandment with a promise – that it may go well with YOU and that YOU may enjoy long life on the earth" (Ephesians 6:2-3, NIV).

Nothing could be simpler. To dishonour ones parents is suicidal.

"For God said, 'Honour your father and mother' and 'Anyone who curses his father or mother must be put to death'" (Matthew 15:4, NIV).

Many lives have been shortened and many have been sent to an early grave for having disregarded this injunction by God. I must emphasise however that the first reason to honour your parents is your welfare. Put it this way: After God, you next, then others.

Let us look at one more New Testament verse. The entire Old Testament is summarised in this verse.

"Jesus said to him, 'You shall love the LORD your God with all your heart, with all your soul, and with all your mind.' This is the first and great commandment. And the second is like it: 'You shall love your neighbour AS yourself.' On these two commandments hang all the Law and the Prophets" (Matthew 22:37-40, Emphasis mine).

Love your neighbour AS yourself? Notice that verse said you are to love your neighbour 'as yourself,' not above yourself, not in place of yourself.

"Be kindly affectionate to one another with brotherly love, in honour giving preference to one another" (Romans 12:10).

In preference, you can decide to offer your space to someone. Even after you have given that space, it remained your space that you gave away. You are inferior to none and no one is superior to you. When you prefer your brother's comfort to yours, you are simply honouring him.

We make people who would not give beyond the biblical requirement feel less holy or even unrighteousness. So they give with their hands but not with their hearts.

Let me share with you the story of Ananias and Sapphira in the book of Acts. The announcement went forth like this, "Brethren, we need your help to look after the needy amongst us. These people are new converts who have turned their backs on the world to follow Jesus and we won't let them down. Nothing is too big or too small." then the donations started flooding in; big ones, small ones, expensive ones, cheap ones, clothes, shoes, foods, and many more. You name it; everything was brought.

The simple call soon turned to something else, 'fund-raising extraordinaire.' It became a competition. Who would bring the best? Who would offer the most? So people started selling their boats, horses, houses, and landed properties. Those who held on to their houses, contrary to people's expectations were made to feel less spiritual.

Soon entered a couple, "Minister, guess what? We sold our land." "Really, for how much?" replied the minister. (Of course the minister knew about property prices and was in the boat business himself). After he was told the price, the minister shouted "you liars."

Bang! Ananias fell on the floor and died. A few hours later, Sapphira 'conspirator-wife' also went down on the floor. She was declared dead on the spot, just like her husband. They died because they lied about the value of the money declared against the profit they made on the sale. They did not die because they did not sell their property, neither were their deaths a result of not giving all the equity they made on the house. This is what the minister said;

> *"The property was yours to sell or not sell, as you wished. And after selling it, the money was yours to give away"* (Acts 5:4, NLT).

No, they didn't have to sell their house. It appears that they were not compelled to do that as much as they were not forced to give any of the equity on the house. The money was theirs to keep if they wanted to but as soon as they made up their minds to give it, they couldn't lie about its worth.

It's in your power whether or not to release what belongs to you. Do not allow people to put you on guilt trip because you did not give to satisfy their ego. You only give because you are being led by the Holy Spirit to give, not because you want to prove you also can give substantially.

Looking after 'number one' (after you have fulfilled your responsibilities to God) involves spending good time looking after yourself outside your savings. You must create time to refresh and replenish – taking regular holidays for instance, just to engage in the mundane. That includes spending quality time with those dearest to you – your spouse and children.

You must create time to refresh and replenish; taking regular holidays for instance, just to engage in the mundane.

It is also a time to play, eat out, watch TV, listen to music, and read good clean fictional stories. Many people haven't done that for a long time. All their lives, they have been spending their time looking after other people's interest, putting others first.

You need to look after yourself. Your time is now. I am not talking about wasting time. I am saying that you should take reasonable, responsible, and sensible breaks. Even Jesus left the crowd to rest. He would notice a gathering crowd and think it was time to leave. This is a lesson our generation need to learn.

Looking after number one also includes your responsibilities to your parents and even your relatives. No one can teach this value better than Jesus and Apostle Paul.

> *"But you say it is all right for people to say to their parents, 'Sorry, I can't help you. For I have vowed to give to God what I could have given to you.' You let them disregard their needy parents. As such,*

you break the law of God in order to protect your own tradition'" (Mark 7:11-13, NLT).

"But anyone who won't care for his own relatives when they need help, especially those living in his own family, has no right to say he is a Christian. Such a person is worse than a heathen" (I Timothy 5:8, TLB).

Allow me to make this emphasis again - your time is now: to serve and service yourself. If you keep serving and servicing others without stepping aside every once in a while to replenish and look after your own interests, you will soon end up needing help like those you are helping. Life is about giving and receiving. If you keep giving without receiving, you will soon be depleted. Your resources will soon be used up and you may not even find help from those you helped. So take time off to look after yourself.

Other People Next

Let us go back to the Bible. Commandments six to ten are for others. From Exodus 20:13-17 or Deuteronomy 5:17-21 we deduce the following:

6. *You shall not murder.*

7. *You shall not commit adultery.*

8. *You shall not steal.*

9. *You shall not give false testimony against your neighbour.*

10. *You shall not covet.*

"For the commandments, 'You shall not commit adultery,' 'You shall not murder,' 'You shall not steal,' 'You shall not bear false witness,' 'You shall not covet,' and if there is any other commandment, are all summed up in this saying, namely, 'You shall love your neighbour as yourself.' Love does no harm to a neighbour; therefore love is the fulfilment of the law" (Romans 13:9-10).

You would not want to commit adultery with your neighbour's wife or husband if you claim to love him or her. Neither would you murder your neighbour, steal his property, bear false witness against him or covet his belongings. You would not like someone that says he loves you to do any of those to you either. You would think he is a hypocrite because what he profess is not in line with his action. The last five commandments are summarised in the statement, *'You shall love your neighbour as yourself."*

We have a major assignment to the less privileged. Jesus did not turn a blind eye to the needs of people. He only stepped aside to refresh and later return to ministry. He helped them and we should. If we do not, our religion is irrelevant and unacceptable.

> *"Pure and undefiled religion before God and the Father is this: to visit orphans and widows in their trouble, and to keep oneself unspotted from the world"* (James 1:27).

My point here is this: your ministry is divided into three. There is ministry to God and there is ministry to your neighbour and right in the middle of that is your responsibility to yourself and your immediate family.

Your ministry is divided into three. There is ministry to God and there is ministry to your neighbour and right in the middle of that is your responsibility to yourself and your immediate family.

God will never ask that you should place the ministry to your neighbour above your ministry to yourself and your family. In actual fact, the requirement before you minister to others is to first show your ability to manage your home. Therefore, other people come after you and your family.

You are probably feeling better already, but if that is because you've been looking for excuses not to give or bless others, then you've got me wrong. This is not a book to encourage you to block the flow of God's blessing to you. If you stop giving, the flow of material blessing will be hindered. I want you to give not for man's award but for God's reward. The Bible is full of God's wonderful promises and rewards for extending God's goodness to others.

> *"And let us not get tired of doing what is right, for after a while we will reap a harvest of blessing if we don't get discouraged and give up. That's why whenever we can we should always be kind to everyone, and especially to our Christian brothers"* (Galatians 6:9-10, TLB).

> *"Feed the hungry and help those in trouble. Then your light will shine out from the darkness, and the darkness around you will be as bright as day. The LORD will guide you continually, watering your life when you are dry and keeping you healthy, too. You will be like a well-watered garden, like an ever-flowing spring. Your children will rebuild the deserted ruins of your cities. Then you will be known as the people who rebuild their walls and cities"* (Isaiah 58:10-12, NLT).

"Be generous, and you will be prosperous. Help others, and you will be helped" (Proverbs 11:25, GNB).

When I speak about others, they include your Church family, friends, neighbours, work colleagues, business partners, study group, and extended family members.

The conclusion is this: if you have your priorities in the proper perspective, you will take good advantage of the opportunities God brings your way. Do not let your opportunities slip by because you feel obligated to serve others. The time is now. Your time is now. Maximise the moment.

Key Points to Remember

1. Your time with God should be foremost; second to none and non-negotiable. This includes time to pray, time to study God's word, fellowship with brethren and attending Church.

2. Look after yourself. You must create time to refresh and replenish. Take regular holidays to engage in the mundane. Spend quality time with those dearest to you - time to play, eat out, watch TV, listen to music, and read good clean fictional stories.

3. Look after other people; we owe them this responsibility. These include your Church family, friends, neighbours, work colleagues, business partners, study group, and extended family members.

Lightning Source UK Ltd.
Milton Keynes UK
UKOW051705020113

204277UK00007B/18/P

9 781907 734441